POEMS FROM A COUNTRY PARISH

Rev. John W. Friesen, PhD, DMin, DRS
drsfriesen.com

POEMS FROM A COUNTRY PARISH

Produced by
Virginia Lyons Friesen, PhD
drsfriesen.com

Dedicated to congregations

I had the privilege of serving

in Kansas, USA and Alberta, Canada

POEMS FROM A COUNTRY PARISH
Table of Contents

3

On Prayer, 51

4

Sunday School, 63

5

Seasons and Special Days, 71

6

On Family, 91

7

Tributes, 111

POEMS FROM A COUNTRY PARISH

INTRODUCTION

Most clergymen would probably agree that a half century in ministry should provide a few valuable insights regarding planning for an enriched retirement. I think my 55 years in ministry did that for me, and I am now happily retired. I can confidently say with Saint Paul:

"I have fought the good fight, I have finished the race, I have kept the faith" (2 Timothy 4:7 NIV).

My pastoral duties through the decades included a variety of appointments; I was at times a youth minister, an assistant or associate pastor, a part-time pastor, and also a full time minister. I was a full time minister twice, first for five years with the Evangelical United Brethren denomination (now part of the United Methodist Church in the United States), during which time I was also a doctoral student at the University of Kansas. My second stint as a full time minister was for nine months with a fairly sizable urban church in Calgary, Alberta. The balance of my professional training and energy was spent in small rural and urban congregations whose budgets could not sustain a full time minister.

When I first became a licensed (and later ordained) minister, I felt called to emulate the tent-making philosophy of Saint Paul. Translated into action this meant that I would serve congregations on a part-time basis and financially sustain myself and my family by teaching at a university. To that end I attained a PhD degree as well as six other degrees in both secular fields and in divinity studies. I also served as a full time professor at the University of Calgary for 48 years.

There were times when my tent-making philosophy was severely tested. This occurred when I discovered that part-time ministers are typically held responsible for the same roster of responsibilities as full time ministers. These activities included conducting Sunday morning worship services (and sometimes Sunday evening services as well), teaching Bible studies, undertaking home and hospital visitations, and keeping up with church conference demands.

It goes without saying that all clergymen, full time or part time, are generally expected to be available 24/7 to conduct weddings and funerals, as well as to offer counseling or preside over the Sacraments of Holy Baptism and Holy Communion when requested.

During my half century of ministerial service I sometimes found it quite difficult to juggle my university class schedule in order to preside over a wedding or a funeral. Fortunately, my faithful and supportive wife, Dr. Virginia Lyons Friesen, was always willing to transport me to church from university by automobile, while I changed clothing in the back seat of the car! I am happy to report that this responsibility was only one in the series of tasks that Virginia has undertaken during the course of our marriage—all of them fulfilled faithfully in a spirit of strong support.

Juggling two careers can be challenging and/or enriching, and at times even frustrating. Both institutions-- university and congregational service can be quite demanding on one's time. Universities expect faculty members to fulfill a whole host of tasks when not engaged in classroom teaching. These obligations include conducting research, writing up and reporting the results, serving on faculty committees, mentoring graduate students, and presenting personally prepared papers at learned conferences. Congregations, on the other hand, are often quite unaware that clergymen may also have family responsibilities, they may relish a bit of off time, and at times even manifest a desire to be left alone. This harsh reality can influence busy professionals to undertake "off camera activities" that involve watching or engaging in sports, spending time in the wilderness at a cabin, or even relishing the ownership of a sports car or motorcycle!

Perhaps this is why I began to write poetry. This activity provided me an opportunity realistically to describe congregational life in rhyme, sometimes even engaging in what some might call poetic license. In the meantime I must confess that I also participated in a series of alternative activities that included dabbling in real estate, dirt biking and long distance motorcycling, as well as always having a convertible automobile on hand! If I cannot be forgiven for these "off-campus" activities, I plead for tolerance! I might mention that several other clergymen I have met or worked with during my career may have to join me in hoping for understanding.

The poems contained in this volume were generally penned about experiences or impressions of rural church life. Several of them have appeared in press in various religious and secular publications, but the majority were written for weekly church bulletins or monthly newsletters. A variety of themes are included, most of which are aimed at enhancing appreciation for rural church life.

Happy reading!

Rev. John W. Friesen
Professor Emeritus of Education
University of Calgary
2017

1

Worship and Preaching

SUNDAY CHURCH

It seems to me that if God's Word,
I really want to know,
The thing to do on Sunday morn.
Is to our church to go.

Now some of us it's plain to see,
Have got too much to do,
The preacher doubts, but I declare,
That God must know this too.

Life's little chores o'erwhelm us so,
Our energies they drain,
So who can blame us when we choose,
From worship to refrain?

Now this may sound a little bold,
But God whom we adore,
Will surely count the good we've done,
And even up the score.

If that's the way you calculate,
Your spiritual journey here,
You have a bogus concept, friend,
And can't see things too clear!

—John W. Friesen

BLESSINGS OF WORSHIP

There are none...

If you no motive harbor deep,
Within your inmost soul,
When coming to the house of God,
With no particular goal.

There are a few...

For those who like to join in song,
And fellowship with friends,
Yet basic worth of worship true,
On more than this depends.

There are more...

Reserved for those who come to pray,
To ask of God some things,
However, worship means much more,
It's what a person brings

There are many...

As those well-know who come to church,
Both to receive and give,
And what is more, they're richly blest,
And leave for Him to live!

These are for you...

If you would reap the blessings
Of real sanctuary bliss;
Then tune your heart to God today,
And worship not amiss!

—John W. Friesen

GIVE GOD GLORY

In daily living there's a trend,
For us on only self depend,
No wonder that it's hard to send,
God some glory.

> When trials rise on every hand,
> And when it hard to take a stand,
> In order to our fears disband.
> Give God some glory.

Why is it difficult to see,
That daily we need ever be,
Dedicated—full and free,
Giving God glory.

> Is it because we've never walked
> With Christ, or seldom with Him talked?
> Have we our Savior ever mocked
> With empty glory?

Perhaps our gifts are insincere,
The goal of service seems unclear,
And even church is rather drear,
Producing no glory.

If you an answer to this seek,
To rid your heart of faith so weak,
You'd like to reach a mountain peak,
In spiritual glory.

Try taking just a little time,
And set your mind in spiritual clime,
Do this and it won't seem a crime,
To give God glory.

The formula for Christian zest,
To help us love Christ at our best,
Is just to pray, God does the rest,
He reveals His glory.

So take a moment now and then,
To show your thanks to God in heav'n,
And you will praise with meaning, when,
You give God glory!

—John W. Friesen

THE MORNING'S GLORY

O billowed cloud, O morning mist,
Expel thy lustered hue,
Thou glorious sunlight, shine thy rays,
For day has come anew!
          Thou dandelion, thy golden crown,
          Lift high in pride today,
          Thy radiant, brilliant, glory shows
          That God brights morn this way!
The meadowlark and warbling thrush,
Announce that night has fled,
Sing on, ye gentle saints of song,
A happy day's ahead!
          There's little with this glory can
          Compare, too easily,
          For it from God's own hand doth flow,
          Composed Divinely.
A similar state can be achieved,
When we let Jesus lead,
Our spirits change, our goal's revamped,
A happy time indeed!
          Neglect not God's great gift to us,
          For when you Christ receive,
          A new day dawns—and morning comes,
          If you will but believe!
—John W. Friesen

BECAUSE HE'S GOD

The ways of man have ever shown,
 Him finite, frail, and flawed,
Will God His love on man bestow?
 He will, because He's God!

The Bible folk were vessels chose,
 Yet idols did applaud,
But God forgave them when they asked,
 He did, because He's God

The early Christian martyrs bore,
 The Roman's chastening rod,
Yet God was with them—gave them grace,
 He did, because He's God!

Religions oft the Lord reject,
 Their minds with thoughts are strewn
Of man-made gods, and yet He loves,
 He does, because He's God!

Believers too, the Lord deny,
 His holy name defraud,
But He'll renew, refill, restore,
 He will, because He's God!

—John W. Friesen

SINGING LIFTS THE SOUL

On Sunday morn we go to church,
We pray and read and sing,
And many blessings can be ours,
It bears on what we bring.

If we our hearts will open wide,
And take in everything,
Then God will surely speak to us,
When we begin to sing.

The hymns, the chants, the choruses too,
Are sung with zest and zing,
The more we put our hearts in it,
The better we all sing.

We lift our voices loud in praise,
Make sounds in everything,
We clap our hands and homage give
To Jesus Christ the King.

The Lord our worship always loves,
So let our voices ring,
Across the church and heaven-bound,
Now come, and let us sing!

—John W. Friesen

A GIFT OF PRAISE:
DEDICATION OF A NEW CHURCH ORGAN

Again, it's Sunday in the land,
And people everywhere will go
To worship God, with praise in heart,
That He His blessing might bestow.

Our purpose here is manifold,
We'll sing and praise with spiritual lift,
But also with a thankful heart,
We'll dedicate a lovely gift.

This charming organ in our church,
Exemplifies a lasting love,
For as it's played throughout the years,
It'll radiate a heav'nly love.

An organ offers sound supreme,
Its quiet, soothing music wells
The soul in worship, quells the fears,
And stirs the heart through lyric swells.

We'd like to offer special thanks,
To those who made this gift so fine,
Few instruments such merits boast,
As furnishing both calm and spire.

The music of this hallowed thing,
Can comfort so the heavied soul,
Restore the heart to spiritual height,
And melt the stand of firmest bold.

And so this pearl of sound we've found,
Its peals of lilt will long endure,
These will give warmth to heart and mind,
And set our spiritual path more sure.

And so may God this vessel bless,
Re-consecrate the church this day,
And may our worship sweeter be,
Because we've been enriched this way.

—John W. Friesen

A "WORSHIP" EXPERIENCE

I came to the church one day to pray,
And hear what the pastor had to say,
The church was filled with folks that day,
With looks of contentment, joy, and dismay,

I wanted to concentrate on the word,
I wanted relief for my weary soul,
I opened my ears and focused my eyes,
With worship my immediate goal.

To the right of the church there were children,
Unattended by parent or friend,
They were rolling a ball to each other,
I was tempted my guidance to lend.

Near the front sat an interesting couple,
A man with his wife by his side,
His mouth was stretched open in slumber,
His snoring he cared not hide.

A youngster was sprawled with a hymnbook,
And glared at the songs and the notes,
Busily scratching and scribbling,
Evidently was "feeling his oats".

I gazed at the section of young folks,
And was struck by the sight of one's face,
All puffed up a wrigglin' and wranglin',
He chewed gum as though in a race.

We concede true worship's commitment,
Takes hours we spend each Lord's Day,
So should we blame people for trying
To launch a more diversive way?
Personal Application:

I guess that my purpose in worship,
Is fully my heart consecrate,
I really would like to achieve this,
If I could at least concentrate.

Perhaps where we fail in our worship,
To appreciate solace and peace,
If we did, our praise and our worship,
A more attentive spirit would release.

I'm going to try harder next Lord's Day,
My interests to better control,
If I try not to notice diversions,
The service may benefit my soul.

—John W. Friesen

THE MODEL PREACHER

A pastor and his preaching,
Are seen as close entwined,
In fact, some view the pulpit,
A wee bit like a shrine.

A hearer told a preacher,
His style was very warm,
He proudly told his missus,
His boast was true to form.

The wife winced at his bragging,
As daily he would rant,
Till one day she had had it,
"To hear this more, I can't!"

As time went on, the preacher,
Again received a pat,
A woman said his preaching,
"Stirred hearers where they sat!"

The word she used was "model",
A preacher true to form,
The pastor liked the concept,
Now he was great and warm!

The preacher's wife grew worried,
Her mate was growing proud,
Not only was he bragging,
His voice was getting loud.

She told him to do research,
On "model," on the net,
He did, and found the meaning,
Was not what he'd expect.

A model is a shadow,
Imitation of the real,
The preacher took the message,
And ended his big spiel!

Whenever you feel lofty,
Check out the compliment,
Your good looks and your talents,
May not be heaven-sent!

—John W. Friesen

THE CRISIS IN PREACHING

Too much of our preaching, I think,
Reflects a mere flickering blink,
At the problems our people might nurse.
Our pastors see much that's amiss,
So they scold and they holler and hiss,
Their anger they're quick to disperse!

> **Our pews** may be loaded with folks,
> Whose burdens we don't comprehend,
> Because we're so busy 'gainst sin;
> Our hearers go home unrelieved,
> Their hearts have no respite received,
> The sermon no spirits did win.

Our Lord in His preaching tried hard,
The growth of folks' sins to retard,
But His words were directed to need.
The people accepted His word,
They acted on what they had heard,
Because of the way He would plead.

> **O Father**, in heaven above,
> Teach preachers to mingle in love,
> Their deeds and the words that they speak.
> May their spirits and desires be pure,
> To comfort and help, not injure,
> For Christ said, "Blessed are the meek".

—John W. Friesen

A SHORTAGE OF MINISTERS

A problem causing much dismay
Within the church today,
Is one that cannot easily, be solved,
It's sad to say,
It seems that leaders hardly know,
Just where the trouble lies,
But we need preachers, quite a few,
Before the priesthood dies.

The problem is of great concern,
To all who follow Christ,
We need to have more ministers,
Regardless of the price,
This difficulty is not new;
It's come upon us through
The years, because we've failed,
To challenge worthy youth.

One cannot thoughtlessly declare
That this or that be blamed,
The cause of this dilemma,
Should every Christian shame,
Perhaps all noble members,
Their motives ought to search,
Instead of proudly watching,
From a lofty distant perch.

Our Lord His twelve disciples,
Imploringly beseeched,
That they should pray the Father,
If folks were to be reached,
To send forth many workers,
The harvest field to till,
Despite their many efforts
To do the Father's will.

But even here, their duty,
Was not reduced at all,
Because their consecration,
Was more than just a call,
Christ told His loyal followers,
That they as well must go,
And bring the Gospel message,
Workers are needed so.

Today we're short of ministers,
Because we're so involved,
With things of earth—our jobs, our sports,
Just things that will dissolve,
Few faithful Christians do their job,
In praying for laborers,
But even praying Christians must
Love their own neighbors.

So let us stop our fretting,
About this quandary now,
And heed the call of Jesus
And humbly 'for Him bow.
Besides this let us search our hearts,
About our future plans,
It might be God wants us to preach,
To meet these grave demands.

—John W. Friesen

OUR NEW CHURCH HOME

Written on the occasion
of having accepted
a call to a new congregation

The last few months have quickly passed,
It's hard to believe time goes so fast,
But it was when we first arrived,
To live among you, and to strive
To be your pastor, and to preach,
That we with you might others reach.

At first our task was "just for now,"
We got to wondering just how
We'd manage, on a certain day,
Our assignment ceased, and we couldn't stay,
But somehow God arranged that we
Might labor with you, happily.

We'd like to thank you for the way,
In which you showed you'd have us stay,
The thoughtful gifts of food and things,
Are not forgotten--our memory clings
Not to the gifts, but to the thought
That you our satisfaction sought.

Quite clearly you have shown your care,
In all the ways you sought to share,
Our home repairs, with sparkling walls,
The windows cleansed, and fresh-scrubbed halls,
All these reveal conduct so rare,
They're proof of Christian love and care.

So thank you, friends, and may Godspeed,
You in next year, and fill your need,
Today we to you cheerfully lend,
A hand that we might jointly send
God's message forth, and others bless,
So they might His dear name confess.

—John W. Friesen

A MODERN PARABLE

I have a parable to tell,
I heard a fellow say,
About a certain friend of mine,
I tell it with dismay.

No matter where he goes to church,
Or what the preacher's theme,
He shrugs the message off his back,
And says, "It's off the beam."

You take last Sunday, by the way,
The parson said, "Forgive".
My neighbor never blinked an eye,
Man, what a way to live!

Now every single soul in church,
Knows what this fellow done,
He sold me grain that wouldn't grow,
No matter how much sun.

It made me mad for 'most a year,
I rarely spoke to him,
Boy, he's got a lotta nerve,
His Christian light is dim.

I wonder why folks act that way,
When sermons get across,
They seem to sit there petrified,
Neglecting Jesus' cross.

The man had told his parable,
But hadn't hit grass roots,
Why is it when the gospel's preached,
It seldom fits our boots?

—John W. Friesen

2

Bible Studies, and Theology

THE GOSPEL OF MARK

Mark's Gospel truly is a book,
That tells what Jesus taught,
And if we study on His words,
We'll surely learn a lot.

Christ healed the sick, and fed the poor,
And called on folks to lead
Their people into righteousness,
And God's true message heed.

The crowds reacted to His words,
With joy and hope, in chorus,
But some resisted what He said,
And chose their own resource.

He told folks parables of truth,
Of lessons they should know,
He told of seeds and mustard trees,
And how the Kingdom grows.

And then one day, He on the cross,
Was hung to die for sin,
His life was gone, but heav'n is ours,
His dying lets us in.

So read the Book of Mark today,
Its truths will lift your soul,
You'll understand that God loves you,
And wants you to be whole.

—John W. Friesen

BEATITUDES IN JAMES

I've often wondered when I read,
The Bible ere I went to bed,
Why God had not said more—
On topics not quite clear to me,
On subjects that are dear to me,
Those that I much adore.

In Matthew's Gospel, I declare,
The best of scripture is found there,
As "Blesseds" they are known;
So few in number though they be,
They've stamped our lives indelibly,
We've claimed them as our own.

So as I read yet other works
where spiritual truth so often lurks,
I tried to find them there;
I searched the Psalms and Proverbs too,
I read the prophets, Job and Ruth,
But badly did I fare.

I turned my Bible to the end
And started reading once again,
The New Testament 'tis called,
I scanned the books that Paul had penned,
I read them to the very end,
I felt that I had fouled.

I wanted to conclude my quest,
I felt that I had done my best,
No other writers had
These words impressed upon their minds,
At least not any I could find,
I felt it just too bad.

And then one day, whilst browsing round,
The Book of James I felt I'd found,
Its truths I then did delve,
The "Beatitudes", as line on line,
Out from the pages seemed to shine,
In four: verse six through twelve.

Submit to God in humility,
And you bless, just wait and see,
The apostle told his friends,
Our God will give you of His grace,
From you He'll never hide His face,
On faith it all depends.

Resist the Devil, he will flee,
Draw nigh to God and you will see,
That He'll draw nigh to you;
Humble yourself before the Lord,
He is above all else adored,
And should be by you too.

Speak not evil of your brother,
Treat him as you would another
Who may have given you—
A share of wealth, or rank or place,
To him you gladly show your face,
Your brother is God's too!

These are the "Blesseds," James does spell,
And in our hearts the truth must jell,
Until our Lord's return;
For if we truly Christ adore,
To spiritual heights desire to soar,
Then let us of Him learn.

Christ left an impact here on earth,
The Gospels tell His holy birth—
And life until He rose;
Then James and others just like him,
Lest Jesus' teachings might grow dim,
His words to us expose.

I read God's word with renewed zeal,
New spiritual treasures I'll unseal,
Like those in James' book;
It may well be, in quiet repose,
That I'll find others, just like those,
If I but only look!

—John W. Friesen

ODE TO THE BOOK OF JUDE

Deep nestled in God's Holy Word,
Lies Jude;
Sadly neglected, seldom stirred,
In solitude;
Untouched because of brevity,
Ignored;
Assessed in spirit of levity;
As if bored.

The purpose of this concise verse,
An appeal;
Delivered briefly, clear, and terse,
And very real;
Its content readily demands,
Attention;
Its depth and historicity commands,
Retention.

Neglect not carelessly this pearl,
Oh, please;
Endearing truths you will unfurl,
Them seize—
And clasp them firmly in your heart,
In confidence;
For those behave who these can't find,
In diffidence.

Too often blessings we've forsook,
In haste;
By skipping swiftly through God's Book,
Such waste;
Thus many truths lie hidden there,
Hardly touched;
A spiritual gold mine, we could share,
Jude is such!

—John W. Friesen

THE BIG QUESTION

A question I frequently ponder,
But one that inspires me though,
Concerns the "beginning" of people,
And why God created them so!

One school of thought stresses purpose,
And declares that mankind must obey—
God's centralized plan for the whole race,
With no individual say!

Some persons pay court to the mere chance,
Of folks being made as a thing,
Without any purpose or pattern,
Like a bird that is loose on the wing.

Perhaps we're confusing the issue,
And a simpler, more rational plane,
Would reveal that God wanted some creatures,
On whom He His blessings could rain!

—John W. Friesen

THE "PROBLEM" OF GOD

Some folks have a problem believing,
That God is a person for sure;
So they make up all manner of theories,
And strongly on folks these adjure!

The atheist gives us his viewpoint,
With reverence becoming a saint,
Declaring with words full of scoffing,
"God isn't, He isn't, He ain't!"

"I worship my God in His beauty",
The naturalist proudly declares,
"The trees and the birds and the meadows,
Themselves are the objects of prayer."

The idealist adds to confusion,
With standards he neither can reach,
"You cannot be certain of theory,
No matter how hard you may preach!"

"But first let us clear up our object,"
The philosopher gravely puts in,
"If God is concerned with the universe,
Does He indwell without or within?"

The polytheist's shocked at our "ignorance",
Assuming the Father is One,
"Is there not a god for each substance?
For everything under the sun?"

Wise Solomon wrote in his proverbs,
With words full of meaning and tart,
"The person who doubts God's existence,
Is a fool, and is not very smart!"

I'm sure that our Father in heaven,
Must pityingly look from above,
When He sees all the interpretations,
Folks make of His purpose in love.

God sits not alone in the heavens,
His Spirit doth o'er all prevail,
And still in the heart of the seeker,
He makes His most meaningful grail!

—John W. Friesen

THE GREATEST CHANGE

There's nothing that's strange,
About folks wanting change,
When they realize their state before God;
And the thing they've to do,
Is to sin say adieu,
And bury it deep in the sod.

It is then that one's life,
Ceases malice and strife,
And alignment with Jesus begins;
Christ's love fills each thought,
And redemption is sought,
In place of the lurings of sin.

Soon God's love surrounds,
And real joy resounds,
The Christian reflecting God's grace;
All past guilt is gone,
Since to Christ's we've been won,
In service we then take our place.

—John W. Friesen

IN LOVING OBEDIENCE

From early childhood we've been told,
That sharing standards we should mold,
Of things entrusted us to hold—
In loving obedience.

And yet somehow, as growing came,
We shared much less, and felt no shame,
We made a list of those to blame,
Failing in obedience.

When adulthood quickly came to be,
We gained in wealth so easily,
The church we served so feeb-i-ly,
In neglected obedience.

We blamed our attitude on those,
Who Jesus failed, and riches chose,
We said they were not on their toes,
But feigning obedience.

O Christian, when will you awake,
And rightfully your duties take?
And strive excuses to forsake,
And ensue obedience?

There's little wonder in this world,
That slander at the church is hurled,
It will, till giving is unfurled,
In responsive obedience.

Our aim on earth is folks to win,
To steer them from a life of sin,
That they may life for Christ begin,
In joyful obedience.

Now come, let's not go on this way,
But with a yielded spirit say,
I dedicate my all this day,
In loving obedience.

—John W. Friesen

THE URGE TO ERR

Occasion'ly, when things go wrong,
My friends I do offend,
If only once, might be forgiv'n,
But then I do it again.

It's not that I'm unsociable,
Or do not need a friend,
It's just that when I vex someone,
I always do it again.

This is a universal fault,
It's really quite a trend,
That when folks say some nasty things,
They always do it again.

I wonder if it's only that,
Folks can't their habits mend,
Or do we only rationalize,
So we can do it again?

Now those who've "got religious faith",
Should not their spirits spend?
Because they really can be changed,
And not offend again.

There are some things worth doing again,
Like ent'ring in your den,
And there, with faith in Jesus Christ,
Praying and praying again.

I think the way to beat this thing,
Is asking God to send,
His Holy Spirit to daily guide,
Instead of now and then!

—John W. Friesen

RECIPE FOR LOVE

I like a melancholy scene,
Occasion'ly, it's quite a cure,
For when its lines I contemplate,
I sense emotion, deep and pure.

Disconsolation in a song,
Oft leaves my soul in spirits high,
For when I bear with others' plight,
My heart in sympathy doth sigh.

I think I like depressing books,
Where tales of misery are told,
For if I disregard such trials,
My spiritual life may start to mold.

So show me hunger, sadness, pain,
And make my heart in mercy writhe,
Unless we know another's plight,
We'll not in love our substance tithe.

A shriveled, isolated soul,
Oft has no basic knowledge of,
The human suff'ring in this world,
Hence cannot sympathize in love.

The remedy for such an ill,
Consists of empathy and grace,
For when we fathom human pain,
We surely earn in heav'n a place.

—John W. Friesen

LASTING VALUE

Sometimes the sweetest things in life are short,
Like speeches.
I hope my pastor always thinks of this,
When he preaches.

There is some advantage in getting things done,
When they're tough!
And oh, how we love to finish our tasks,
When they're rough!

We hurry and scurry and worry along,
To get done;
And when we've completed we feel that we've won,
A bright crown.

Why is it that people are always so rushed?
Where are we going?
It could be that we the whole world want to own,
And it's showing!

But wait, there must be things that are like a tough climb
—like maturity;
And spiritually, we should be giving some time,
To eternity.

Our life is brief, the Scripture points this out,
Like a vapor;
Our flame burns low and dim and hardly seen,
Like a taper.

With this in view, we should for the future,
Lay a plan;
And this we should involve ourselves in doing,
As soon as we can.

If our goal is ever to be more like Christ,
It'll take time;
Each act, each thought, each word, and each goal,
Is a climb.

Yes indeed, some things can be done quite fast,
But they pass;
Those that add spiritual dimension take time,
But they last!

—John W. Friesen

THE LIFE CYCLE

Infancy—the **best** of life,
In cradled innocence,
The world its torrid temptings pours,
The babe makes no defense!

Childhood, and the **zest** of life,
Bursts open into view,
Searching, believing—so eagerly,
Yet sweetly, as the dew.

Youth, and here the **test** of life,
Engulfs life's precious young,
Each meets the challenge, soars away,
To earth's far corners flung!

Adulthood, the **rest** of life,
Reflects one solemn thought,
Regain what's lost, and find anew,
What's given can't be bought.

Eternity, the **quest** of life,
Has ended, finally,
The trust betrayed, or faithfully kept,
Decided Divinely.

—John W. Friesen

THANKS, I'D RATHER NOT!

A line that makes one weary,
And people use a lot,
Is really just a brush-off,
It's, "Thanks, I'd rather not!"

Can you imagine someone,
Whose health with illness fraught,
His doctor offers solace,
Says, "Thanks, I'd rather not?"

Or take a needy student,
Whose finances are naught,
A scholarship refuses,
With, "Thanks, I'd rather not!"

And yet when God extends us,
Without our being aught,
A blessing, through some service,
It's, "Thanks, I'd rather not!"

It seems we've got warped values,
For Christ who us has bought,
May heaven's door refuse us,
With, "Thanks, I'd rather not!"

—John W. Friesen

TAKE TIME TO BE FOOLISH
A Parody

Take time to be foolish, Speak not with thy Lord,
Abide with Him never, And ignore His word,
Bypassing His children, Join those who are weak,
Forgetting in nothing, Your carvings to seek.

Take time to have pleasure, The world rushes on,
Spend time in enjoyment, With leisure alone,
By looking to pleasure, Like it you shall be,
Your friends in your conduct, A vacuum shall see.

Take time for your schooling, Let it be your guide,
And run not before it, Whatever be tide,
In joy or in sorrow, Still follow your school,
Folks watching your conduct, Will know you're a fool!

Take time to make money, Be calm in your soul,
Each thought and each motive, Beneath its control,
Thus led by the "green stuff", To fountains of lust,
You soon shalt be fitted, To return to the dust.

—John W. Friesen

LINES PEOPLE USE

A poem should always be in rhyme,
But this one doesn't work,
I cannot match their deeds in verse,
When folks their duty shirk.

A case in point is quite well known,
It's obvious in a fellow's tone
Who thinks he's whipped, and so he'll moan;
"OK, if that's the way they want it,
I'm never coming to church again!"

Another line to which we're prone,
In similar vein, is easily shown,
Upset, we'd like to pick a bone;
"Well, if she thinks she can run the whole show,
I'll just stay at home and let her!"

A silly line, we oft condone,
From coast to coast this habit's flown,
A Christian's "knife" can deeply hone;
"Well, if they don't like my idea,
see if they're going to get me to help with that project!"

And have you heard the ringing phone,
Where gossip high in wind is blown,
And voices long in volume drone;
"Did you hear what he said?
Just because so-and-so acts that way is no reason
To take it out on me!"

There's still another petty show,
Which we assume when asked to go,
To service in another zone;
"Ask somebody else; they can do it better than I can.
Besides, it's much easier to sit back
And criticize others when I'm not involved!"

I'd like to take a long-term loan,
On every pious, fruitless drone,
Who has the nerve to wail and moan;
"I just try to do my little part. If it's not appreciated,
There's little I can do about it!"

Well, now it's out--care to disown,
A pastor who assumes this tone?
"He's got his nerve, we won't condone;
A man like that shouldn't be in the ministry.
He can't he control his emotions?
That's not Christian. Of all the nerve!"

—John W. Friesen

TWILIGHT

Twilight; the landscape melts in silhouette,
Its profile sketched in lines of black,
Ethereal symmetry reveals no lack,
But day's delights can't be brought back.

Twilight; the throb of another's pulse quieted,
The painful prod of life's short breath,
Immortality, the hope at death,
Fond memories the sole bequest.

Twilight; in every reminiscence faced,
A dusk in every deed performed,
There's no recapturing those deformed,
Man's only hope—in God transformed.

—John W. Friesen

3

On Prayer

PRAYER

Prayer:
To us is like an avenue
That opens up to clearer view
God's heavenly grace—to us endue,
His mercy rare.

Prayer:
Is like a magic, lifting force,
That stems from holy sacred source,
And helps us heartily endorse,
Our Christian fare.

Prayer:
Our Shangri-La—from daily woe,
To gain release from stress, our foe,
But yet to God, why don't we go?
Life's wear and tear.

Prayer:
Through sorrow, grief and fiercest pain,
Though vexed with fright, fear and disdain,
What is it helps, so faith won't wane?
Our Father's care.

Prayer:

Is like the breath of glowing spring,
With spirit, as when children sing,
It lifts our souls, so we can bring,
To God our cares.

Prayer:

Neglect not heaven's finest gift,
God hears our call, His answer's swift,
He'll give us sure a spiritual lift,
Enjoin in prayer!

—John W. Friesen

MEETING GOD

I Met God...

When in the brilliant realm of budding,
Bursting spring there rose—
A fragrant soft aroma—
So gloriously in package stowed,
In petals soft, with brisk green leaf—
That to my wond'ring eye it showed
That God had this created!

I Met God...

Amid the feel of ice and snow,
When desperate railed the storm,
Among the trees, now hid beneath
Great mounds of white—
High-borne their leaves, and out of sight;
Left only swirling sounds of mourn;
To me this majesty revealed!

I Met God...

In every season, every clime;
He's everywhere around,
And though folks often fail to see
Or hear His heav'nly sound,
And though it takes a little while,
A moment, and He can be found,
For our God is everywhere!

Have you met God?

Just gaze into a cradle-bed,
And note that tiny breath,
For through that entire life,
God guards, until eventual death;
In sickness, problem, grief or pain,
The Scripture clearly saith,
"That God cares for us!"

—John W. Friesen

A TIME ALONE

There are those times, I do regret,
My problems no solutions get,
I like Elijah, in his cave,
(To whom the birds provision gave),
Feel much downcast, and right put out,
My mind is filled with stress and doubt,
And then I come alone a while,
And rid my soul of all things vile,
My God provides His inner peace,
My desperate struggles quietly cease.

When certain persons leave their place,
For worship seldom show their face,
Another tries to steer my course,
With various tactics, even force,
My neighbors bother not with church,
For God, they show no need to search,
Then, when I come alone a spell,
My frustrations God doth quell,
Then, I remember Jesus said,
"Your conduct must be spirit-led!"

This age has parented pressures sore,
Instead of less, they're becoming more,
Our social schedules reek of plans,
We scarcely hope to meet demands,
The younger set has no recourse,
But take our path, and it endorse,
If only we could pause a bit,
And calm before our Savior sit,
That He might help us see His will,
And us with His own Spirit fill.

—John W. Friesen

THE LORD'S PRAYER

$\mathcal{O}$ur dear loving Father in heaven above,
We hallow Thy name, in obedient love;
May Thy kingdom come, and may Thy will be done,
On earth as in heaven, as though they be one.

$\mathcal{G}$ive us this day, Lord, the bread we require,
Forgive us our debts, we do humbly desire;
That we may our fellowman also forgive,
And without trying temptings, we pray let us live.

$\mathcal{D}$eliver us from evil, O Lord, in this hour,
For Thine is the kingdom, the glory and pow'r;
We pray that forever thy mercies might shine,
That folks might acknowledge Thee, Father Divine.

Amen.

—John W. Friesen

AN EASTER PRAYER

Eternal God, our Refuge Thou,
We humbly seek Thy face,
We pray Thee, bow Thine holy ear,
And grant us now Thy grace;
We recognize our weaknesses,
We know that we are flesh,
And numerous are the pitfalls,
By which we are enmeshed.
      We need Thy caring, helping hand,
      To guide us through this life,
      For many are the lures and traps,
      That lead to sin and strife;
      We know, O Lord, that peace will come,
      If we but learn to rest
      On Jesus' all-sufficient grace,
      And give Him of our best.
           It seems we know the answer, Lord,
           To settle our estate,
           We place no stock in human powers,
           We need to learn to wait
           Until Thy Spirit, overwhelms
           Our stubborn, selfish goals,
           And aims and plans for self-decay,
           And love can fill our souls.

                   —John W. Friesen

THANK YOU, LORD, FOR RAIN

Thank you, Lord, for rain,
A sweet and heavenly gift,
And when it comes, it gives a lift,
To every field and plain.

Thank you, Lord, for rain,
For when we concentrate,
And all its riches contemplate,
That it's a gift 'tis plain.

Thank you, Lord, for rain,
Without it this old earth,
To leafy green could not give birth,
And folks would plant in vain.

Thank you, Lord, for rain,
E'en though we haven't prayed,
Too easily our faith is frayed,
Thanks Lord, for watered lane.

Thank you, Lord, for rain
In many ways its salve,
Is like the life that Jesus gave,
When He endured the shame.

Thank you, Lord, for rain,
For its full fresh, clean scent,
Sure comes from Thee, 'tis heaven-sent,
For blessing, and for gain.

Thank you, Lord, for rain,
And for the Christ who gave,
In similar fashion, folk to save,
His life, His pain, our gain!

—John W. Friesen

A PRAYER FOR HOLY COMMUNION

Be present at our table, Lord,
And may this solemn deed,
Inspire each participant,
Thy words to truly heed.

Thy presence at our table, Lord,
Reminds us not to judge
Another's life, lest we ourselves,
Be found to bear a grudge.

Thy presence in this holy deed,
Will make the moment right,
Without it, we might find ourselves,
Enacting something trite.

Be present at our table, Lord,
And may we from this place,
Go happily, with blest assurance,
That we have seen Thy face.

—John W. Friesen

4

Sunday School

TEACHING SUNDAY SCHOOL

I'd like to see more loyalty,
Than what has been the rule,
Concerning an important task,
Like teaching Sunday School.

Some think that all you really need,
Are balls of yarn and spools,
And all you have to do is play,
And that is Sunday School!

And other teachers I have known,
Think they are really cool,
They read an hour to their class,
And call that "Sunday School".

And then there is the lecturer,
Who'll vocalize and droll,
While all the class sits meekly by,
Enduring Sunday School.

I think a teacher in the church,
Should really be God's "tool".
A servant in a blessed role,
Teaching Sunday School.

The secret of a well-taught class,
Is when someone will pool
Their resources, with Christ as Guide,
In teaching Sunday School.

In every aspect of the church,
The Christian needs renewal,
And in particular it's true,
In teaching Sunday School.

If you're involved in this great task,
Just think it o'er, and you'll
Responding turn to God for aid,
In teaching Sunday School.

It's music to a Christian's ear,
And to our joy adds fuel,
To hear some youngster proudly say,
"I love my Sunday School!"

—John W. Friesen

PARTIAL THINGS

A lesson book and blackboard brush,
Don't make a Sunday School;
A teacher with a loving heart,
Is far a better rule!

A deacon's bench, and choral strains,
Aren't really all the church;
But Christians filled, with God's great love,
Would climax such a search.

To witness of the Father's care,
Is part of Christian walk;
But earnest love for all God made,
Surpasses any talk.

Why be content, with partial things,
When Jesus made it plain;
If you would have, real Christian love,
Don't spend your time in vain!

The Bible take, and meditate,
Let prayer flow from your heart;
For God will bless abundantly,
If we will do our part!

—John W. Friesen

SUMMER BIBLE SCHOOL

I used to think when just a boy,
That life was full of joy,
When birthdays came and Christmas too,
And I'd receive a toy.

But I discovered as I grew,
That life could hold much more,
I learned of values and beliefs,
And what my life was for!

On Sunday in the house of God,
And at my mother's knee,
I found all that which satisfies,
Exists eternally.

And then one day I went to church,
Each day for one whole week,
They called it, "Summer Bible School",
New Bible truths to seek.

We talked of how the earth was formed,
And why the Savior came,
These topics we discussed a lot,
And I did Jesus claim.

My parents were absolutely thrilled,
That I could learn so much,
But most of all, while I was there,
I felt the Savior's touch!

I'd like to thank that little church,
And all the teachers too,
For helping me to see that Christ,
Guides little children too!

For now that I am grown, I see,
That if it not been,
That God found me while young in life,
I might have strayed in sin.

—John W. Friesen

A CREED FOR YOUTH

Lined up in cue to challenge youth,
And test their faith and wisdom too,
Are churches in this land of ours,
Of various kinds, and blends, and hues.

The Methodists, Episcopals,
The Baptists, Lutherans, Mormons too,
And many churches less well known,
Each claims to be the one that's true!

Each seems to have its "coat-of-arms",
Sometimes the very name's the cue,
But often, in reality,
Their special traits they overdo!

What should inquiring youth today
Concerning faith, aspire to do?
Would it be wise to trust in fate,
And every structured church eschew?

Perhaps a few criteria,
At this point could be offered through,
The contemplation of what's dear,
When forming a doctrinal view.

Whatever stance you finally choose,
Blend in some love and interest too,
When you meet folks, who disagree,
Then lend an ear, and get their view.

So often in this life we find,
That faith and practice, not mixed true,
Present a picture not quiet clear,
Of what it is that we should do.

Let's not our brand of creed flaunt high,
Lest we a hurtful path ensue,
Instead of furthering God's plan,
We offer man-made schemes in lieu!

—John W. Friesen

5

Seasons and Special Days

SPRING

'Tis spring, and all the world's aglow,
With flowered field and fen,
The winter winds that fret and blow,
Have been silenced.

In spring, our fancy turns to love.
And we seek happiness,
Our intense wants are far above,
Our possibilities.

In spring the earth blooms forth with zest,
In sparkling colors bright,
And many joggers strut their best,
With idealistic motivations.

With spring the calendar reveals,
That Easter time is near;
But Christian conduct oft conceals,
Its true significance.

What does your heart reflect in spring?
Perhaps a mundane wish;
This season through us ought to bring,
More relevant acts.

At this time Jews the Passover lift,
Mohammedans their fast,
And fullest bursts God special Gift,
His precious only Son.

So spring a richer season is,
Than others in the year,
Because at that time on the cross,
Christ wrought salvation dear!

—John W. Friesen

SEASONS OF LOVE

In spring youth's fancy turns to love,
And all the world seems right,
Warm sunshine, flow'rs and pink-lit skies,
Indeed, the whole day's bright!

In summer when the moon glows bright,
And day's extended long,
Young couples stroll with hearts alight,
And all the world's a song.

The autumn leaves prepare a stage,
For love that asks adieu,
And night comes quickly, ending day,
But love will still prove true.

The glist'ning, whitened fields and glen,
Bear witness, winter's here,
Warm hearth with embers all aglow,
Permit a love most dear.

All season love, untouched by clime,
Permits a love that's true,
All season love, endures through time,
And has a special hue.

Beyond the pale of earthly life,
There's Love, can't be described,
Divinely made, the source of care,
Is by the Lord prescribed.

Our heav'nly Father's caring love,
Makes pale the things on earth,
Its essence is our constant goal,
It has a matchless worth.

—John W. Friesen

MOTHERHOOD

Most sacred role in human life,
    By God Himself decreed,
Observed in all its blessedness,
    A privileged role indeed!
Tis motherhood, we're speaking of,
    The gift of giving birth,
Having a part in this event,
    Endorses women's worth;
Enveloped in the mind of God,
    From earth's creation day,
Released when Eve did birth her sons,
    And proudly them displayed;
Hence women ever were enrolled,
    To propagate the race,
Oft-times this duty is abused,
    And held in ill repute,
Obsessed with cares and many wants,
    'Tis easy to forget,
Do not this honored role neglect,
    You'll owe to God a debt.

—John W. Friesen

MYSTERIES OF EASTER

We know not how the cross,
Was formed, or how it looked,
We're not exactly sure,
Just whom the last glance took
Before the Lord His grave,
Enjoined—was laid away,
Or even who it was,
That rolled the stone that day!

We know not how it was,
That Christ could rise again,
Nor can we hope to try,
This miracle explain;
E'en Thomas could not dare,
To say that he it knew,
Though Christ permitted him,
To test if it were true.

There're many things we so,
Desire to understand,
But God has chose to leave,
Them all, within His hand;
The Alpha and Omega,
Beginning and the End,
On whom could we expect,
Much better to depend?

Of Easter there is much,
That Christians cannot say,
We understand for certain,
It might be best this way;
For God demands our faith,
When trusting in His Son,
And this explains just why,
Our logic's overrun!

The moral of this poem,
In Jesus' deed is shown,
When He the blind man healed,
His method was unknown,
The man was plagued by friends,
"How come? What was the key?"
He said, "I am not certain,
I just know I can see!"

—John W. Friesen

THE CHRIST OF THE HYMNS

The hymns of Easter speak of Christ,
"Behold the Lamb of God!"
"The Blood Will Never Lose Its Power!"
"We're Saved by Jesus Blood."

"All Glory Laud and Honor" speak
Of *"The Old Rugged Cross"*,
Because of Jesus' will to die,
We gain from His great loss.

"There's Power in the Blood" of Christ,
"There is a Fountain Filled..."
And Calv'ry covers all our sins,
No shame to us is billed.

These truths will grip our hearts and souls,
If we, *"Kneel at the Cross,"*
When we *"Survey the Wondrous Cross,"*
Through faith, we're cleansed of dross.

But praise the Lord, *"Our Savior Lives!"*
"Up From The Grave He Arose",
"You Ask Me How I Know He Lives?"
His love He daily shows!   —John W. Friesen

A SOURCE OF JOY

It's difficult, I know it is,
For some to understand,
That when the toils of busy life,
Rise up on every hand—
That some are glad, completely so,
Their daily life this shows,
The reason is because the Lord,
Has conquered all their foes.

At Calvary, 'twas there one day,
That victory was wrought,
The Son of God with His own blood,
Our own redemption bought,
And then He rose, with pow'r o'er death,
Eternally to live,
Our source of joy is based on this,
That God His Son did give.

When we have claimed this inner peace,
That Christ alone supplies,
Then joy is ours, abundantly;
It comes as no surprise
To see the Christians happily,
About their daily place,
With radiant life and cheerful look
And smiles upon the face.

Our God has promised He'll supply,
Our every daily need,
And more than that,
He'll guide our steps and carefully us lead—
To greener pastures in His word,
That we like Christ might be,
Revealing love in all our deeds,
That folks may Jesus see.

 To keep our constant source of joy,
 That comes from heav'n above,
 We'll fill our minds with things
 Of truth, of honor, and of love,
 It helps to bear in mind with Paul
 That we must firmly stand,
 And stable be, and not give up,
 Because the Lord's at hand.

—John W. Friesen

THE CROSS: A MUTUAL RESPONSIBILITY

The world today surveys the cross,
And thinks of those who hoisted it,
As men of vile repute, who stood
Out from the world—outcasts, misfits;
But any thinking Christian knows,
That they who made the Savior bear
The cross, did not alone their crime commit,
Not they, but we too put Him there!

On yonder hill, His foll'wers stood,
The women, John, and those who came
To bear respect, to God's own Son,
And sympathize with His great shame;
But they too, in their hearts did feel,
That only those who lift
The cross, in actual deed were vile,
But no, they too, caused Christ to die.

In ev'ry century since the first,
In writings, messages and prose,
The scathing mobs and jeering priests,
Have suffered literary blows,
By good-intending theologues,
Who thus attempted them to smear
With blame, for putting Jesus there,
Thereby implying they were clear!

It happens, Christian, in each age,
We point our fingers critically
At others—those from various walks
Of life, and do this jeeringly,
Too oft we fail to see the truth,
That God has uttered in His book,
"For all have sinned and fallen short,"
And this we'll know, if we but look.

—John W. Friesen

AUTUMN LEAVES

When summer's heat has disappeared,
And all the crops are in,
Another harvest waits its turn,
And silently begins.

The rustling on the wind-swept street,
Announces autumn's here,
The colored leaves that dot the ground
Remind us, winter's near.

God's harvest is the autumn leaves,
Each with a unique shape,
A color, size, and bent its own,
That sets the world agape.

Then gently, slowly, one by one,
Each leaf makes its debut,
Until assembled, multifold,
The lawn's a glorious view.

God's harvest gradually completes.
Almost unseen, unheard,
Until at last the task is done,
And every leaf has stirred.

God's harvest sparks no turbid roar,
Unlike machines men make,
And yet its power sweeps the earth,
Transforming in its wake.

The autumn leaves, neglect them not,
But contemplate their lot,
It may well be that you will learn
A less'n not soon forgot.

—John W. Friesen

AUTUMN ASSESSMENT

Somewhat abashed, we realize,
That autumn has arrived again,
And to the conscientious mind,
This season special rapt has when
A definite bent is made to learn,
Its denotation for our time,
For when you stop to think, you'll note,
It's time to check our spiritual prime.

Reluctant quite, and disinclined,
Describes the habitude of some,
When they are broached to fellowship,
And to our special gatherings come,

Still others, greet the thought of these,
Occasions to reflect on life,
To measure, analyze, and search,
To calm the soul of inner strife.

It's strange that such a range of mind,
From just one congregation springs,
That from a "unity" should come,
A heart that halts, and one that sings,
Perhaps it's true that scriptures ring,
With truth and painful meaning deep,
Reminds us that it still is true,
As man does sow, so shall he reap!

—John W. Friesen

DECEMBER

It's plausible that every month,
Presents a flavor, quite unique,
Not seasonal alone, this bent
In other character may be.

December, it is said so oft,
Delivers winter's chilly blast,
The swirling snow and frosty sleet,
Convince the world that summer's past.

Yet this bespeaks another vein,
Existent not in climate though,
For if this month's true secret would
Be understood, then deeper go.

Consider where the twelfth month lies,
It catches on the very end
Of every year, and therein can
A profound truth, be found to fend.

A person's life is nothing more,
Than contemplation of our years,
Each starts and ends, a beat in time,
Until the process disappears.

A thinking soul should contemplate,
And set up goals for each new stride,
The final month should be the time,
And this December does provide.

And so each month has its own end,
But when comparisons are made,
Though some may stress a milder clime,
December's will not easily fade.

—John W. Friesen

HE CAME

A child is born,
Gentle, sweet, and meek,
The cross, His goal,
The Savior people seek.

—John W. Friesen

THE SAVIOR CAME

The world lay still in quiet repose,
Great hope was in the air,
God's angel came a maid to tell,
She would the Christ-child bear.

The magi waited through the years,
For news of God's great gift,
Then suddenly, His star appeared,
Its light the skies did lift!

The shepherd watched their slumb'ring flocks,
Prepared with staff and rod,
The angels burst the heav'ns in song,
"Go seek the Son of God!"

The Savior came the earth to bless,
The cross His final goal,
His coming offered us God's best,
And peace to every soul.

—John W. Friesen

A COUNTRY CHRISTMAS

Christmas in a country church,
What's unique about this scene?
Well-worn pews and wooden cross,
Walls need paint; the budget's lean,
Does the aura mold the spirit?
No, it can't our yearning wean!

Expectedly, the church resides,
Statured near a gravel road,
Luring wearied souls to prayer,
Historic, and 'tis God's abode;
Thoughts of worship draw us there,
Disregarding rural mode.

Not the nature of the place,
Nor the draw of its repose,
Buildings can't determine faith,
Nor our weariness depose,
Help comes from a higher plane,
God in mercy heals our woes.

Country, city, acreage lot?
Rural wins by far the game,
Why this happens seems quite clear,
People give the city blame,
Perceiving urban-ness as weak,
Thinking such a life is shame.

Sentiment; the country lure,
Let it not your incline be,
Seeking God in any clime,
Fosters much a better plea,
God, eternal in His stance,
Always welcomes bended knee.

—John W. Friesen

CHRISTMAS EVE CANDLELIGHT SERVICE

On Christmas Eve, in our small church,
When everything is bright,
The candles glow with special warmth,
It is a lovely sight!
Then solemnly, we celebrate,
The Holy Sacrament,
Our hearts are tuned to hear God's voice,
As on our knees we're bent.

> The atmosphere is awesome,
> And, there's beauty all around,
> The church is one—united all,
> Because His peace we've found;
> And then the lights are darkened dim,
> The sanctuary filled,
> With joyous voices, candlelight,
> The church is peaceful, stilled.

So every year we wait for this,
Our Christmas Eve respite,
And every year it brings anew,
A special, glorious, sight.
Dear Father, God, we thank you so,
For Jesus, Savior dear,
His Love fulfills our greatest hope,
At Christmas Eve each year!

—John W. Friesen

CHRISTMAS CELEBRATION?

Oh, you can take your puddings,
And gifts, and tinseled trees,
And with them you'll find most folks,
Will be entirely pleased.

They'll think that it's been Christmas,
When all's been said and done,
And all the fret and worry,
Has settled with the sun.

But what is left to witness,
Of Christ's first advent here,
When all our busy botherings,
Ignore God's gift so dear?

—John W. Friesen

6

Family

WHO SO FINDETH…PROVERBS 31:10

Wise words cannot always explain things,
Like the meaning of Lemuel's thought,
That finding a wife who's a treasure,
Is something that cannot be bought.

Most men would prefer to be so blessed,
And I stand right out in the crowd,
I married a wife out of Proverbs,
And I with her am really wowed!

I ponder why God chose to do this,
To bless me with such a good wife,
I try to say thanks to our Father,
By lovingly enriching her life!

—John W. Friesen

DEAR MOM—A TRIBUTE

•Barbara Reimer Friesen 1911-2001•

When May rolls 'round, I think of you,
And all that you have done,
For me, and all the family,
I'm proud to be your son.

For years you struggled on the farm,
And in the city too,
But everywhere we felt at home,
'Cause we got love from you.

No matter what we found to do,
Or where we settled down,
You always prayed and wrote to us,
You ought to get a crown!

So on this Mother's Day we wish
God's best for you each day,
Because you're always there for us,
Means more than we can say!

—John W. Friesen

DAD'S 90th BIRTHDAY—A TRIBUTE

•Gerhard D. Friesen 1903-1997•

We welcome friends to this event,
A special day it is,
Our Dad reached ninety years this week,
This day is really his!

The span of time since Dad was born,
Began before the car,
Before the TV, disc, and chip,
The dollar was on par!

Dad worked a store, the fields, and bush,
He butchered in between,
There was no challenge left untouched,
No scars he hasn't seen.

With mom he raised a brood of five,
And that was quite a feat,
Of course abundance wasn't there,
But always we did eat.

The brood of five has sprung some heirs,
The line just seems to grow,
And if you add the whole score up,
We're dozens now in tow.

Through all their travels, jobs, and moves,
Our parents had just one line,
"Obey the Lord and do His will,"
And things will turn out fine!

So "Happy Birthday" Dad, today,
We wish you all the best,
But more than that, we heartily,
Thank you for your bequest.

—John W. Friesen

A FATHER'S WISDOM

A boy his father asked one day,
"Whence come the seas and sands?"
His father, puzzled, quick replied,
"From God's Almighty hand!"

The boy responded, quite impressed,
"You're such a clever man!"
His father smiled, and wisely said,
"I too, am from His hand!"

—John W. Friesen

MY BOY

•Bruce K. Friesen•

To some his birth was no surprise,
He wasn't much of any size,
To me he really was a prize,
'Cause he's my boy!

I watched him as he older grew,
With parental pride, I'd tie his shoe,
I'd even grin when things he'd lose,
'Cause he's my boy!

I spent good money so he'd learn
Of homework, I'd remind him stern,
I taught him when to take his turn,
'Cause he's my boy!

The time swept by, he soon did leave,
Our home not much thought did receive,
But still in him I did believe,
'Cause he's my boy!

He found a wife, a job and friends,
He learned that life on love depends,
He taught his young to make amends,
'Cause he's my boy!

And then one day my heart was thrilled
My doubts about him all were stilled,
With tears my eyes were quietly filled,
'Cause he's my boy!

I heard him tell his boy of love,
The kind, he said, "that's from above,"
My dad will teach you all 'bout love,
'Cause I'm his boy!"

The years have gone, and I no more,
Can move about beyond the door,
But there us one—makes my heart soar,
And that's my boy!

—John W. Friesen

MY LITTLE CHERUBS

•Karen B. Friesen & Gaylene J. Martens•

My days at times are filled with cares,
I fret and worry so,
Stress problems rise up everywhere,
I know not where to go.

                    Sometimes in busy moments sore,
                         I rush from chore to chore,
              The time runs out, of work there's more,
                    The whole thing I deplore.

When I go home, all tuckered out,
A welcome rents the air,
"Our daddy's home," they shout aloud,
And lead me to my chair.

                 They're three and four, those little dolls,
                        Cherubs in disguise,
                They fill my arms in soft embrace,
                    My daughters, what a prize!

My cares are quickly done away,
My mind is soothed just then,
With joy and pride and happiness,
" 'Cause daddy's home again!"

                 There's nothing more sincere I know,
                    Than love that children bring,
                  It melts your sordid troubles fast,
                    You feel just like a king!

—John W. Friesen

MY FIRST DAUGHTER

•Karen B. Friesen•

Eldest of my daughters three,
Wanted to a teacher be,
Reached her goal as we can see,
I'd like to think she copied me!

Raised a family of three,
Working hard to raise the fee,
To promote her youngsters' glee,
They're as happy as can be!

Faithful in her Christian walk,
She did more than merely talk,
At no challenge did she balk,
Her example makes folks gawk!

Gracious, kind, and humble she,
Few you'll find so honest be,
Finest hostess you will see,
Trusted friend she'll always be!

Thank you, Father, for my part,
Helping give this child a start,
For this privilege, I'll be tart,
She'll be always in my heart!

—John W. Friesen

MORE THAN A DAUGHTER

•Gaylene J. Martens•

Time went on with a new scene,
In a place I'd never been,
A second daughter just arrived,
A new status I derived.

Now a father of two girls,
Sets my mind in a deep whirl,
Who should be so richly blessed?
Time to host a joyful fest!

As she grew to youthful age,
She unleafed a crowded page,
She picked colleges in twos,
Now she didn't have to choose,

Two degrees were in her hand,
To new quests she did expand.
Marriage and three children soon,
Teaching a related boon.

Family soon began to grow,
She to China arranged to go,
Adopted daughters arrived in tow,
Brand new family all aglow!

Seven in the family now,
People often wondered how,
She that schedule handled well,
Strangers couldn't hardly tell!

Still her faith remained intact,
Church support a solid fact,
Family, teaching, rich success,
Doesn't seem to need a rest.

Now a grandma to just four,
I'm predicting there'll be more,
She continues to dispel,
Fear of failure she'll soon quell!

God send blessings, unawares,
A real way He shows He cares,
The gift this daughter represents,
Truest form of God's present!

—John W. Friesen

OUR GIFTED SON

•David J Friesen•

Some people have talents aplenty,
Our son keeps me truly amazed,
He showed his abilities early,
No challenge could deflect his gaze!

He came to our home without fanfare,
His physique was of a slim size,
His gifts were his outstanding feature,
And that's why we call him our prize!

A blacksmith, an artist, and teacher,
In college he really did thrive,
In studies featuring children,
From birth to a child's age of five!

In high school he spent time in forging,
Uniquely developed designs,
On crafts that gave birth to a market,
That featured uniquely forged lines.

Our home has been upscaled by paintings,
Our artist has talent to draw,
Rich oils and bright pastels are featured,
They're viewed in a spirit of awe!

Too often as parents we are blinded,
To gifts God bestows on one's home,
At times these appear in our children,
No need to search "bushes to comb"!

So let's thank our heavenly Father,
For giving us children to love,
It's clearly our duty and privilege,
To emulate that from above!

—John W. Friesen

AND ONE MORE DAUGHTER

•Beth Anne Droppert•

Rich blessings unexpected,
Included one more heir,
This time, another daughter,
A third, so cute and fair!

Once homeschooled by her mother,
She studied with a flair,
Her homework oft included
Cooking; we thought it fair!

A student out of country,
Picked Waterloo with care,
Eventually found a husband,
And ended living there!

We made so many visits,
It seemed like quite the place,
We packed up our belongings,
Now Waterloo's our base!

We now have neighboring grandsons,
Quite often at our pool,
We hope to keep them coming,
The arrangement's really cool!

We'd like to thank our daughter,
For guests who grace our place,
We won't be terribly lonely,
For most folks is the case!

So once more God delivered,
An unexpected gift,
It's essence is quite complex,
For us, a regular lift!

—John W. Friesen

MY THREE DAUGHTERS

•Karen, Gaylene & Beth Anne•

Each culture has its values,
As students learn to see,
Numbers may be sacred,
Some say the number's three!

I've several lovely daughters,
They came to us in threes,
My life's enhanced quite richly,
Deeply blessed by these!

A gift my daughters gave me,
I'm sure you would agree,
Grandchildren numbering eleven,
I hold them on my knee!

These little folks teach lessons,
When they, "Have me for tea,"
These visits are a pleasure,
My hosts serve me with glee!

My daughters have professions,
Mostly they teachers be,
I think their students lucky,
Good teachers are the key!

God often sends folks blessings,
We get them without fee,
For me it's gifted daughters,
I'm grateful for all three!

—John W. Friesen

VOWS TO KEEP

'Twas as a child, I first did make,
A vow that shaped the course
I was to take, throughout my life,
When faith I did endorse.

In simple, childlike faith I came,
My Savior to receive;
The assurance plainly given me,
My burden did relieve.

Another vow, much later on,
Meant much to me because
My name upon church record books,
As a member entered was.

The years passed by and I did shirk,
My duties for the Lord;
Until a sermon gripped my heart,
And God His Spirit outpoured.

I vowed that Christ I'd follow through
Life's battles, long and rough;
And knowing Him as the Great Guide,
He'd give me strength enough.

And this He did, I hardly strayed,
And many victories claimed,
I did my best to honor Christ,
And glorify His name.

A fourth vow changed my entire life,
When with a glowing pride,
I stood before the minister,
To claim my beloved bride.

Together we repeated vows,
Our rings exchanged in trust,
And to the union earnestly,
We pledged our solemn trust.

It wasn't long, it seemed to us,
That once again we came,
To promise faithfully to keep,
A view not quite the same.

A little life had come to us,
A child, a son, and heir,
We brought him to the church that day,
To dedicate him there.

We promised that we'd faithfully
This child for Jesus raise,
That when he'd adulthood enclasp,
He also God would praise.

One other vow I made to God,
I stood alone that day,
My family in the assembly stayed,
Supportively to pray.

This sixth vow in its substance was
Most sacred and esteemed,
To me its requisites were such,
I hardly worth was deemed.

"I challenge you", the bishop said,
"The glorious truth to preach,
The church uphold, its saints renew,
And folks for Jesus reach."

And still another vow I've made,
This seventh must be kept,
And daily as I rise from sleep,
Its challenge should be met.

It deals of faithfulness to God,
In every routine task,
With neighbors, friends, and business chores,
For uprightness, I ask.

Each time I frequent church to pray,
And when I sing His praise,
And also when His feast is served,
I might reveal His ways.

These seven vows I'll keep to God,
The last eternally—
Is binding so that when I act,
My peers might Jesus see.

A vow is sacred, should be kept,
Its base intent is deep,
But when you make a vow to God,
He'll help that vow to keep.

—John W. Friesen

7

Tributes

A BRIEF, SWEET GIFT

Ah, the lessons children teach,
When we ponder how they love,
They exemplify the kind,
Radiating from above.

God in mercy to mankind,
And to show His depth of grace,
Created children, let them live,
On the earth, in every place.

There to bright the spirits of parents,
And to let them, daily see
All dimensions of their trust,
Love and truth—sincerity.

Another truth is shown today,
God to us, His jewels, does lend,
When their task on earth is done,
Draws them to Himself again.

Thank you, God, for this brief gift,
We will seek to comprehend,
The lesson you would have us learn,
The message that this child did send.

So thank you, God, for (his/her) brief stay,
We know you called (him/her) back again,
Till the day we join with (him/her),
We trust daily in your plan.

We will strive to make our lives,
Qualified for heaven's face.
For we see heav'ns beckoning call,
In the grace of this small face.

—John W. Friesen

A TRIBUTE TO A CHRISTIAN BROTHER

The first book of the Bible states,
The nature of man's sojourn here,
Threescore and ten, the Lord declared,
And seldom more, shall man's years be.

And so, as though to test his faith,
The Lord permitted peril and pain,
To hamper, haunt and hinder him
Yet lend him aid to heaven gain.

Today we honor such a man,
He was our brother and our friend,
And through his life he loyally sought
On Christ, his master, to depend.

United with his wife, in faith,
This couple built a home where they
Their family raised, then sent them forth,
To find their place along the way.

Then suddenly, the twilight years,
O'ertook our friend, then gradually,
He victim of an ill became,
That made him bedfast, hopelessly.

And now he's gone, we'll miss him so,
But in the Christian hope rejoice,
For though each person must face death,
Its taste is flavored by our choice.

What is the monument he left?
The greatest possible that be,
For through his life he earnest tried,
To please his Lord and Christian be.

In church he always took his part,
In business place he paid his due,
Within his home, he gained respect,
And earned the love of neighbors too.

Each one of us, God gave a role,
While here on earth we move and live,
May each of us in similar vein,
A model and example leave.

—John W. Friesen

A DEPARTED FRIEND

When life we ponder in our search,
To know, and comprehend its trend,
We sometimes find our best resource,
Is being with a friend.
The poets in their musings deep,
A sordid message once did wend,
They labeled man a forlorn soul,
Could he have had a friend?

In every life, events occur,
With which we find it hard to fend,
A simple cure, a touch that lifts,
Is just to know a friend.
Today we honor a true friend,
Among us she a way did wend,
That gently touched our inmost heart,
She really was a friend.

Some moments at her bed of sick,
I would my ear toward her bend,
And hear her words of faith, of strength,
She really was my friend.
At church her soft and winning smile,
A ray of warmth and peace would send,
And anyone who touched her hand,
Would find she was a friend.

And in her neighborhood, its clear,
Her family she with care did tend,
Those folks who came to know her name,
Discovered her a friend.
What is a friend? It's such a one
—whose life is true, does not pretend,
I've never seen a finer one,
Than our departed friend.

Perhaps the greatest gift we give,
The best of life extend,
Is to another love bestow,
And really be a friend.
When such a message is enclasped,
Perhaps we'll start a trend,
No, that approach its depth achieved,
In our departed friend.

—John W. Friesen

OUR SISTER'S GONE

She isn't here, she's gone to be
With God, in heav'n above,
And this same Lord it is who heals
Our wounds, with tender love;
Quite suddenly, the Lord did bid
Her body to the sod,
The monument she left behind?
"Someone who walked with God!"

—John W. Friesen

A TRIBUTE TO A BROTHER

In carrying out a pastor's task,
There's many a time when he,
Relies on faithful Christians
Who will take the time to be
On hand, to fill that extra place,
And share the load he bears;
Such men and women worthy are,
Of extra special prayers.

It's just a year ago that we,
Laid such a one to rest,
And though he'd protest 'gainst this thought,
I count him with the best,
Not just because he was my friend,
Nor member of my parish,
But simply 'cause in all his ways,
He lived the truths we cherish.

A patient man in all his ways,
Our departed brother was,
And even when things were not too good,
He didn't make a fuss,
"It doesn't pay," he said to me,
"To fret away our lives,
Because that God, when night is done,
The sun lets brightly rise."

And irrespective of the time,
Of year, or what the clime,
When Sunday morn rolled 'round again,
He was in church on time;
In preaching I would glance
Toward the pew he occupied,
And there he was with reverent eyes,
In worship, satisfied.

To worship God meant much to him,
'Twas obvious by the way
He took a part in church events,
And how he day by day
Exhibited a stable walk,
A faith that seemed to grow,
In spite of things that try us so,
In faith he'd higher go.

'Tis not my purpose here to boast,
Nor push to higher plane,
The testimony of a friend,
Whose own life made it plain
That when we place our trust in Christ,
And let Him lead the way,
Our every action shows His will,
Each part of everyday.

Dear Christian, give your best to God;
Don't waste your time in quest
Of earthly things that won't endure,
For when you go to rest,
Your life will stay behind you
As a monument and plaque.
So why not as our brother did,
From Christ hold nothing back.

—John W. Friesen

ODE TO UNCLE HENRY

Through customs we express our lives,
Our deepest woes, our joys our sighs,
And one such thought great truth belies,
"In loving memory."
I'd like to offer such a thought,
In memory of a man who sought,
To practice just what Jesus taught,
And in His memory.

A year ago, God bid him rest,
Life challenged him, he stood the test,
And heav'n was his, God's very best,
A comforting memory.
As "Uncle Henry" he was known,
And by his deeds he set a tone,
That spoke of life by faith alone,
A durable memory.

One summer we had quite a drought,
That it could rain, there was some doubt,
But Henry said the corn would sprout,
An impressive memory.
His faithful testimony stayed,
For from his goal, he never strayed,
He worked, and spoke, and sang and prayed,
A consistent memory.

And sometimes when my tasks seemed long,
I'd visit with my brother strong,
And come away, my heart in song,
A happy memory.
O Christian, it's not what you say,
Or who you are, or what your pay,
It's what you are from day to day,
That builds a memory.

   These lines were penned that we might take
   This challenge for our Savior's sake,
   That as we walk, build in our wake,
   A lasting memory.
   We dedicate these lines to one
   Who ran the race, the crown has won,
   Who drew his strength from God's own Son,
   In loving memory.

—John W. Friesen

A TRIBUTE TO A FRIEND

Its just a year ago today
that we his body laid away,
But with us memories will stay,
Until we meet in heav'n someday;
He tackled every task with zest,
And every duty gave his best,
Till it was done, he wouldn't rest,
A well-done job, his constant quest.

In music our friend did excel;
In church, his talents did dispel,
E'en illness not his joy could quell;
He loved his Lord and knew him well.
Yes, he had faults like all the rest,
He'd be the first to this suggest,
But he these tendencies repressed,
So he for God could give his best.

And in his last days, I did stay
Beside his bedside, day by day,
And there I prayed, that just a ray—
Of hope might come, that he might stay.
But no, God had another plan,
And though it's hard to understand,
We placed the matter in His hand,
Assured that it'd fit His program grand.

The final day came slowly near,
And for the last time I did peer
Upon his face; he didn't hear,
My mournful voice, "He's gone, I fear."
Yes, he is gone, we miss him so,
But we must understand that though
He's gone, we need to carry on,
The church now waits on us, you know.

—John W. Friesen

A TRIBUTE TO A STONEY
(NAKODA SIOUX) ELDER

The Scriptures provide people, "Threescore and ten,"
But sometimes the Lord gives more days,
Today we rejoice that we know such a man,
Our elder is eighty today!

In youth our friend showed very quickly that he,
Rare talents and gifts would display,
His people accepted the role he would fill,
And that's why our tribute today.

Years ago our dear elder a wife did locate,
Her consent was what made his day,
They raised a fine family together as well.
We honor the couple today.

Our elder's rich service is hard to define,
He sings, and he preaches, and prays,
His faithfulness always directs us to God,
We want to say thank you today.

Whenever our people a counselor need,
Or someone to brighten their day,
They call on our brother and he gives a hand,
And that's why we laud him today!

We gratefully offer a tribute today,
Our heartfelt esteem we relay,
To truly a brother, a servant of God,
Who's turning to eighty today!

—John W. Friesen

ODE TO THE CHURCH JANITOR

Sometime folks are quick to decide,
Which church tasks to take in their stride,
So when it's a matter of pride,
They let the janitor do it.

In worship we love to take part,
We pray and we sing from the heart,
But with menial tasks we are tart,
"Let the janitor do it!"

The front door in church has a squeak,
And the roof is beginning to leak,
But because we are humble and meek,
We let the janitor fix it.

Sometimes when our children get bored,
And some of their chewing gum gets "floored",
We're so busy "a-servin' the Lord",
We let the janitor clean up.

At times when we finally quit church,
And feel we've been left in a lurch,
We leave hymnbooks removed from their perch,
For the janitor to pick up.

I realize this sounds a bit horrid,
And his life must be busy and torrid,
But remember we're paying him for it,
So let the janitor do it.

But perhaps on that golden-gate day,
When Jesus determines "our pay,"
He will kindly, selectively, say,
"Just let the janitor in!"

—John W. Friesen

A TRIBUTE TO MISSIONARIES

Across the wide oceans of tumult and rage,
Through forest and frontier they came,
Unarmed, but with Bible and faith in the Lord,
They sought neither fortune nor fame.

India, China, South Seas, and Japan,
The story of Christ did receive,
Without fear, unflinching, undaunted and loyal,
No nation bypassed did they leave.

The men and the women, who took up the call,
Endured many hardships, we're told,
They blazed quite a trail with the Gospel they preached,
And drew souls into the Lord's fold!

Today more are needed to fill in the gap,
To bravely the message declare,
In missions, in service, where'er comes the call,
The message of Jesus to bear!

—John W. Friesen

ODE TO A RETIRING HOSPITAL CHAPLAIN

Philosopher, pundit, and pastor and priest,
Were channels of our chaplain's role,
In comforting people he daily embraced,
Through caring, with mind, heart and soul.

Sick patients, and doctors, and nurses and friends,
Were equally nurtured on "rounds",
Through caring and counseling and "just being there",
His ministry showed no real bounds.

Now as he retires, he'll pick up new skills,
Perhaps golfing will be his new gift,
But time he will spend with folks anywhere,
Will surely provide them a lift!

—John W. Friesen

A TRIBUTE TO AMERICA

With special thanks to the State of Kansas
for my seven years of formal training there.

The French have got their dressing,
Italians, their sauce,
But talk about hamburgers,
America is tops!

The British have their princes,
The Russians their boss,
But U.S. elections render,
Their leaders by a toss!

The Germans' long-haired lyrics,
And Mexican guitars,
Can't drown the country's music,
It's "way out"—like the stars!

No matter where you wander,
On land, or sea, or air,
It's hard to match their GNP,
With countries anywhere.

Of course they have their problems,
They don't this fact deny,
I only hope they solve them,
They seem to really try.

Americans are haughty,
They're brave, they're strong, and free,
And looking to the future,
I hope they'll always be.

—John W. Friesen

A SALUTE TO 4H CLUBS

Written on the occasion of welcoming the locally sponsored
4H club to the Sunday morning worship service at
Stull Evangelical United Brethren Church, Stull, Kansas

A 4H Club is like a hive,

Of active busy bees,

It opportunity provides,

Without excessive fees,

For youth of many areas,

To cultivate their skills,

A chance to find within this world,

Their gift a need may fill.

Clubs take a lot of time to plan,

And adult sponsors too,

But anything of worth at all,

Will drain some strength from you,

Just think in terms of what it means,

For youth to learn the aim,

For which the club so earnest strives,

And utilize the same.

So welcome, 4H members all,

To church this Sunday morn,

And as we worship corporately,

May we the Lord adorn,

Not just with words and joyous song,

But application of

Club motto and the glorious truth,

That Christ's our Blessed Lord!　　—John W. Friesen

ODE TO A HUNTER

I rode into the forest one day,
My gun was on my arm,
My horse was fresh, my eye was sharp,
The sun shone bright and warm;
The birds released their songs of joy,
The branches snapped behind,
A perfect day, alert I rode,
Big game was on my mind.
Then, suddenly, I caught the rein,
And bid my steed to pause,
I loosed my gun and left the stirrup,
Elated, tense I was;
Before my eyes a buck stood tall,
His head held proud and high,
His antlers glistened in the sun,
And fire was in his eye!

I pulled my rifle to its place,
And squinted through the sight,
My fingers curled the trigger hard,
I pulled with all my might;
The gun resisted my attempt,
No bullet shook my arm,
The buck stood straight—the safety catch,
Had saved his life from harm.

In haste, I sprang the safety catch,
And drew my aim once more,
This time my finger's grasp was limp,
Once more, there was no roar;
The gun was silent, I was moved,
I hastened to my steed,
I felt that God had intervened,
The buck still paid no heed.

I've gone a huntin' many times,
My bounties vary wide,
But this time though I didn't shoot,
I felt real good inside;
That moment when my gun refused,
Because of my mistake,
I saw that buck, had time to think,
His life I couldn't take!
Life holds its lessons quite in store,
Releases them at will,
And we can learn some everyday,
There's many out there still;
For me this day I treasured up,
That nature's wonders are,
The gifts of God to be admired,
To cherish, not to mar.

—John W. Friesen

A PLEA FOR UNITY

A problem troubling folks of late,
Is how our world so thrives on hate,
Not many treat each other straight,
Nor worry 'bout God's Golden Gate!

There are some folks, on any date,
Will torment others with their bait,
But there's a sin that has no mate
'Tis undiluted, stainless hate!

A youngster greedily heaps his plate,
A man of wealth thinks he is great,
A worker shuns his regular rate,
But worst of all, is man with hate.

'Tis really an abominable trait,
One wishes it could in a crate—
Be shipped away by one-way freight,
To hell's defiled and torrid gate.

But God permits the ways of hate,
For folks to pry and prey and prate,
In hopes that some will choose to wait,
On God, that He may compensate.

Our future is not left to fate,
Salvation, God did demonstrate,
In Scripture, did delineate,
The way to heaven's open gate.

So leave the path of earthly hate,
The ways of sin, do remonstrate,
Just take the Word, and contemplate
And hate will vanquished be.

—John W. Friesen

WHO SAYS THAT FRIENDSHIP CANNOT LAST?

In quiet solace, undisturbed,
As quick and calm the years have passed,
Two nations, unified have dwelt,
And shown that friendship long can last.

Canada and the U.S.A.,
Whose flags hang high on coupled mast,
A symbol of a mutual bond,
A trust that lingeringly will last.

The borders of these sovereign states,
Together stretch o'er land so vast,
But still the contract has not waned,
Who says that friendship cannot last?

A parallel, the forty-ninth,
Winds on through forest and field engrassed,
Its charted path, is just a mark,
Of something greater, unsurpassed.

At times new leaders fill their posts,
Oft unprepared, some true, some chaste,
In spite of this, the bond has stood,
Who says that friendship cannot last?

The world today reflects unrest,
And some of war have felt the blast,
Still these two states no quarrels have,
They have a trust that firm will last.

Canada and the U.S.A.,
The future, present, or the past,
A monument of brotherhood,
Who says that friendship cannot last?

—John W. Friesen

A TRIBUTE TO CANADA

On the occasion of
Canada's 150 Birthday
July 1, 2017

Ocean fronts and mountains tall,
Wheated fields, and flush with lakes,
Temperatures, of longest range,
Winters cold, and summer bakes.

Citizens of wide array,
Representing countries from afar,
More arriving every day,
Newly come, but treated par.

Schooling reaches 'cross the land,
Most have college like degrees,
Literacy, a national goal,
This defines our nation's creeds!

Politics, a national game,
Everyone's an "expert" sage,
Opinions represent full range,
This is true of any age!

Choosing where we came to birth,
Not a choice for us to make,
Grateful for God's personal choice,
Thanking Him, and for His take.

Canada's century and a half,
Is quite brief, compared to most,
But her citizens have shown,
Accomplishments of which to boast.

Born in this most northern clime,
I have chosen to adjust
Myself to God's Divinely choice,
Because in Him I place my trust!

—John W. Friesen

ABOUT THE AUTHOR

A Native of Saskatchewan, John W. Friesen, PhD, DMin, DRS, is Professor Emeritus of Education at the University of Calgary and an Alberta Certified Secondary Social Studies teacher. He is the author or co-author of more than fifty books on religion, spirituality, philosophy of education, multiculturalism, and Indigenous studies. An ordained minister in the All Native Circle Conference of the United Church of Canada, Friesen served congregations in Kansas and Alberta for fifty-five years.

John is married to Virginia Lyons Friesen, PhD., an Early Childhood Education Specialist, and they have five grown children and thirteen grandchildren. Having recently retired from ministry and teaching, they moved to the Province of Ontario to settle.

Some of John's related publications include:

Snapshots of Anabaptist Communities—Mennonites, Amish, and Hutterites Plus Doukhobors, a Former Neighbor, Blurb, 2017.
Legends of the Elders: Vols. One and Two (with Virginia Lyons Friesen), Blurb, 2016.

Canadian Society in the Twenty-first Century, 3rd edition (with Trevor W. Harrison), Canadian Scholars' Press, 2015.

Native North American Theology Through a Christian Lens: Comparisons and Contrasts, Blurb, 2014.

Meaningful Moments in Ministry: 50 Years, 20 Denominations, Friesen Press, 2014.

Could You Live This Way? Would You Live This Way? An Illustrated Compilation of Idealistic Experiments in North America (with Virginia Lyons Friesen), Detselig, 2011.

And Now You Know: 50 Native American Legends (with Virginia Lyons Friesen), Detselig, 2009.

What's Your Church Like, Compared With Nine New Testament Models? (with Virginia Lyons Friesen), Xulon, 2007.

Canadian Aboriginal Art and Spirituality: A Vital Link (with Virginia Lyons Friesen), Detselig, 2006.

We Are Included: The Métis People of Canada Realize Riel's Vision (with Virginia Lyons Friesen), Detselig, 2004.

Aboriginal Spirituality and Biblical Theology: Closer Than You Think, Detselig, 2000.

Do Christians Forgive? Well, Some Do, Borealis Press, 2000.

Perceptions of the Amish Way (with Bruce K. Friesen), Kendall/Hunt, 1996.

The Community Doukhobors: A People in Transition, 2nd Ed (with Michael M. Verigin), Borealis, 1996.

When Cultures Clash: Case Studies in Multiculturalism, 2nd ed, Detselig, 1993.

Introduction to Teaching: A Social-Cultural Approach (with Alice L. Boberg), Kendall Hunt, 1990.

The Helping Book, G.R. Welch, 1982.

People, Culture, and Learning, Detselig, 1977.

Religion for People, Bell Books, 1970.